D0123701

Introduction

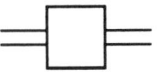

S ome people believe in ghosts, some don't, some are not sure, and others just don't care.

What is a ghost? The Reverend William Rauscher writing in his book *The Spiritual Frontier* says, "The question is rather like asking: What's an animal? Animals come in all shapes and sizes, as mammals, birds, fish, and reptiles (as well as the duck billed platypus, that oddity that doesn't fit in anywhere) and range in appearance from the cuddlesome calf or bear cub to the fearsome crocodile or boa constrictor. Ghosts are similarly diverse." *The Random House Dictionary* defines a ghost as "the soul of a dead person, a disembodied spirit imagined usually as a vague, shadowy or evanescent form as wandering among or haunting living persons."

Those who seriously study the phenomena of ghosts define them simply as the spirits of people, places, creatures, or objects. They say a place is haunted if a spirit is felt, heard, sensed, seen or, smelled. A ghost may appear in its former body or it may be sensed by an odor associated with the person— a lady's favorite perfume for example. A ghost may be present when something physical—a picture, a book, a dish moves without a natural cause such as a vibration or a slammed door. Often the temperature in a place where a ghost is believed to be drops. The space will feel cool and damp like the atmosphere in a cave.

The words "ghost," "spirit," and "entity" are generally interchangeable. When a medium—a person who goes into a deep sleep called a trance—is used to contact a ghost, the words "spirit" or "entity" are frequently used in reference to the personalities who sometimes speak through the medium's voice. Some researchers use mediums, many don't.

If you mention the words "ghost" or "haunting" in a group of people, you may observe a variety of reactions. Some will laugh, possibly even sneer, to think that a reasonably intelligent person would consider such a subject seriously. Others will shudder, hoping you won't mention it again or that you will quietly go away. A third group may question you to determine what you know. This final group of listeners may nod their heads knowingly because they are familiar with the subject and may have experienced a ghost or two.

All the events and experiences related in this book have occurred in the Greater Delaware Valley—that is Philadelphia and its environs. And, to use a common expression, these are just the tip of the iceberg. Every area has its tales or legends about ghosts, hauntings, mysterious happenings, and eerie places. However, places that are recognized as "haunted" are generally very normal looking.

If I detailed every haunting that has been reported to me this would be a multi-volume work. Space dictates that I elaborate on only a few of the most compelling. One such tale related to me by a woman named Marcella. I met Marcella at a party, and she told me that a month to the day after her husband was killed in an automobile accident, she went to bed in the evening, turned out the light, and lay on her left side as she had done for years. In a few minutes, she felt someone move into the bed beside her and an arm went around her waist. This was something her husband had done for many years. Terrified, thinking an intruder had come in, Marcella leaped from the bed screaming and ran into the hall where she bumped into her sister who had been wakened by the yell. Her sister cautiously looked into the darkened room and saw that one side of the bed was undisturbed. Even so, the police were called and searched the premises—no signs of an invader were found.

When the Drexel Hill household was quiet again, Marcella, who had been comforted by her sister, settled down uneasily. Gradually she became aware of the scent of her husband's after shave lotion. Then she had a thought—had he been the one on the bed? The movement had been exactly like that he had made for years. Slowly, in a voice soft with tears, she tried to tell him not to scare her but that she missed him. Her husband's ghost, if that was what she experienced, visited her for seven months on the anniversary of his death—then no more. Marcella believes he came to help her adjust to his sudden departure and to ease his own transition.

In many of the reports in this book, names have been changed to provide privacy. Except for public places, addresses too are vague. Is this type of protection really necessary? Unfortunately the answer is yes. Parts of my home and garden were destroyed by curious seekers when my property was shown on television. Places open to the public should be treated with respect. Rarely, if ever, do ghosts appear on command. Many people who wish to experience a ghost never do. It seems to happen primarily to the unsuspecting.

Finally, a personal note. My psychic experiences have enriched my spiritual experiences and beliefs. I now know the human spirit has eternal existence. To quote William Rauscher again, "If a saint hears angelic voices, it's a spiritual experience; if a psychiatric patient hears voices, angelic or otherwise, it's probably schizophrenia. One experience bears spiritual fruit, while the other is a symptom of spiritual disintegration. The fruit is the test."

As a result, the deaths of family members are not devastating. I know their spirits continue but on other planes. I have been able to counsel and console other people in their grief. When someone reports an experience with a ghost to me, we try to evaluate the experience to learn if it really was that or if there is another logical explanation. Knowing I won't laugh, or think them stupid, many people share their experiences with me. Some are fun, some are very moving and others are questionable.

Happy reading!

1

Joseph Pickett Returns to New Hope

On the banks of the Delaware River north of Trenton, New Jersey lies the picturesque town of New Hope, Pennsylvania. It's well known for its theatre, the Bucks County Playhouse, its great variety of shops, craft houses, and restaurants. It has been, however, long recognized as an artists' colony. The names of Henry Gasser, Lloyd Ney, Ranalph Bye, and especially Joseph Pickett are known to connoisseurs of both modern and primitive art. Joseph Pickett is also accepted by some people as a local ghost.

Pickett owned and managed a grocery story on Mechanic Street two blocks above the Delaware River. He lived in an apartment on the second floor. The house faced the Tow Path House, across the street, and sided on the canal. Although the store provided Pickett with a living, painting was his love. Today he is best known for his primitive paintings such as Manchester Valley and

Coryell's Ferry. Although Pickett died in 1918, he still seems to be amusing himself in his former town.

The Picket House on Mechanic Street in New Hope has been home to several artists and shops.

One winter day a few years ago, Betty, a woman who lived in an apartment in the Pickett House with her family, was in her kitchen beginning dinner preparations. Her infant daughter was asleep in the nursery, while her three-year-old, Billy, was playing nearby. A noise from the bedroom area startled her. Could her husband have returned from work without her hearing him come in? He usually called as he entered and then went to the bedroom to remove his coat and hat. Turning to her son, Betty asked him to go see his Daddy. Billy raced away toward the bedroom.

"Mommy, Mommy! There's a man in your room" Billy shouted as he ran back down the hall toward her.

"Of course," she answered, "it's your daddy!"

"No! No!" he exclaimed. "It's not Daddy! Come, see!"

Holding his hand, Betty led her son toward the bedroom. At the door she stopped suddenly. There was an unknown man in the room, and he was sitting on the edge of the bed on the far side. Turning aside, she pushed her son behind her to protect him. When she looked back toward the bed again, the man was gone.

"Where is he, Mommy? Where did he go?", her son asked repeatedly. Still holding him behind her, Betty carefully looked around. She kicked at the door, but no one was behind it. Cautiously the woman stepped to the foot of the bed so she could see the other side. No one there! She backed out of the room and reached for the nearby telephone.

She called a friend who lived near, telling her an intruder was in the apartment but she couldn't find him although she had spotted him once.

Betty gave the operator a friend's number. When Jean answered, Betty spoke rapidly telling her an intruder was in the apartment. She and Billy both had seen him in the bedroom, but he had hidden somewhere in the place. She asked Jean to find Danny, the local police officer, who could generally be found in the coffee shop on Main Street. "Then come here quickly...please," Betty urged, before she hung up.

Still holding her son's hand, Betty backed down the hallway toward the kitchen. She could see the closed nursery door so she knew he had not gone in there. She could also see the steps leading to the outside door so she would know if he tried to flee.

"Who's the man, Mommy? Where is he? Where did he go?" Billy continued to repeat his questions.

It seemed like hours but actually only about fifteen minutes had passed when Betty heard footsteps on the porch. Then she heard Jean calling her name.

Jean came in followed by Danny who was carrying a drawn gun.

"All right now", Danny called, "everything is okay. Where's the robber?" Betty pointed to the bedroom door.

"He hasn't come out, so he still has to be there!" she said.

Carefully leaning against the door, Danny peered into the room. He looked all around then checked under the bed, behind the door, and in the closet. He opened the window and looked outside even though the apartment was on the second floor. Meanwhile, Jean was searching the other rooms, turning on lights and looking into closets. Then she stopped and turned to Betty who was still clinging to her son.

"Wait a minute," she said "There can't be anyone here! Danny and I just came in. It's been snowing all afternoon and there weren't any footsteps in the snow on your sidewalk, your stairs, or the porch. If someone came in, he would have left footprints."

"But maybe he came before the snow started and hid all afternoon," suggested Betty.

Danny joined the women. His gun was now tucked into its holster. He assured them that no one was in the apartment.

"I even looked under the old tub" he said.

"But I saw him!" insisted Betty. "And so did Billy! He saw him first and came and told me."

Danny knelt on the floor beside Billy to talk with him, asking the boy to describe the man in Mommy's room.

"He was bigger than Daddy, and he had on red," the boy answered.

Then Betty chimed in. "He was somewhat heavy. I don't know how tall because he was sitting on the bed. He was partially bald—there was white hair on the sides of his head that I could see when he turned away. He wore a red flannel-looking shirt and dark trousers. I didn't notice his feet. His cheeks were kind of red, as though he had been outside."

"Have you ever seen him around town? Or in Lambertville?", Or anywhere else?", asked Danny.

"No! No!" insisted Betty. "He's a total stranger! But he has to be here! Where could he go?"

"Can't answer that," replied Danny. At that point Betty's husband, Jim, arrived home and had to be told the whole story. Then he and Danny checked the whole apartment again. No one was found. Finally Danny and Jean left, sure that Betty and her son had over-active imaginations. Betty was uneasy that night and for several days until the incident receded in her memory.

A few weeks later there was an art exhibit at Phillips Mill, a short distance from town. The work of some local artists was featured. On a Sunday afternoon, Betty and her family visited the Mill. In one room were paintings by local artists as well as sketches or simple line portraits of the painters. You can imagine the family's embarrassment when Billy's voice called out, "Mommy, look! There's the man who was in your bedroom!" The boy was pointing to a picture of Joseph Pickett. Betty, too, recognized him. This was definitely the man who had been in her room. But Joseph Pickett was dead. What had she seen then?

She found it almost impossible to believe she had encountered a ghost—a burglar was almost more acceptable.

This was not Pickett's only appearance in the area. As Betty inquired about him in the next few weeks, she learned that he had been seen in town previously, along the Canal, on Mechanic and Main Streets, and by the river. A few months later, Betty and her family moved to another town. The new tenants of the apartment heard footsteps coming up stairs that no longer existed. A couple of years later, Blackburn's Pastures, a shop for custom-made ladies' clothing moved in. Their sewing machine operators had trouble keeping the electric plugs in the sockets because an unseen hand frequently removed them. Later tenants found objects moved, heard knockings on the doors, and the door to the room in which Pickett had painted refused to stay shut. Another resident claimed the wily artist enjoyed locking the bathroom door from the inside.

Pickett seem to be as busy as he ever was. It would be truly special if he painted a new picture, but so far no one has left a canvas ready for him.

2

Fresh Baked Bread

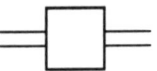

Newlin Mill Park in Western Delaware County contains a grist mill, the miller's home and several restored buildings. They now look as they did in 1704 and later when the new mill was built by Nathaniel Newlin. His father, Nicolas, was a Quaker who came from Ireland to America in 1683 and settled in the Delaware Valley Area.

Before the park was established, Claire and Bill Brown, who had purchased and lived in the miller's house, began to think an intruder was bothering them. Claire vowed that one afternoon when she went into the kitchen, she saw a woman open some drawers and search through their contents. Claire called to her, but the woman disappeared. Was it a trick of light? a shadow? It couldn't be because the drawer was still open. On another occasion, Claire came upon the same woman in a bedroom. She was standing and staring at a dresser. One day Claire saw the woman sitting on the porch steps with her head buried in her hands. Although she seemed to be sobbing, there was no sound. During the next year, Claire saw her uninvited guest about twenty times. Claire generally told her husband about the encounters, but he just shrugged it off and blamed it on her vivid imagination.

Then one Saturday afternoon Claire and Bill returned home from a shopping trip. As they pulled into the driveway, something moving on the porch caught their attention. A woman was pacing there. Her head came half way up the door, so she must have been about five-and-a-half feet tall. Her body was thin and angular, and she wore a dark, dull dress. Her dark hair was pulled back in a bun. She looked toward the car...directly at Claire and Bill... then just faded away. Bill's jaw dropped as he turned to Claire.

"See," she said, "she's just as I told you!"

They both stepped out of the car and hurried to the porch. They searched the shrubbery and carefully opened the door which they had left unlocked. They carefully looked all over the house, but found nobody.

Claire prepared some coffee while Bill sat at the kitchen table. Finally they settled down to talk about what they had seen. Every few minutes Bill shook his head and remarked that he couldn't understand how the woman disappeared so quickly. After he finished his coffee, Bill went outside. He stood beside the car and studied the porch. There seemed no possible way to create the illusion of a woman on the porch with shadows from the trees or porch furniture.

Claire reminded Bill that she had seen the woman many times. Now that he had seen her too, Claire knew it wasn't imagination. She began to talk to Bill about an idea she had been pondering. She had learned of an organization called Parastudy that met in a house nearby which they owned. She was told that they were interested in events such as her disappearing woman. They did no formal investigation of experiences but could identify people who did. Parastudy also was developing a library of books and periodicals about all kinds of seemingly paranormal events. Claire decided to pay them a visit.

At Parastudy, Claire met a dozen people who were interested in her experience. After a lengthy discussion, some group members had suggestions for her.

"What you need is someone who can communicate with a ghost, or a spirit, or an entity, whatever you want to call it. We're almost certain that's what you have. Are you afraid of the woman?"

"No," replied Claire, "but I sure wish she weren't there. She startles me a little. How do I find someone to talk to her?"

Although several recommendations were presented, the best one seemed to be to persuade Dr. Karlis Osis of New York to help. He was described as a person experienced in working with entities. One of the group agreed to contact Dr. Osis to determine if he could and would assist Claire and Bill. Over the next few weeks, many letters and phone calls passed between

New York and Delaware County as arrangements were made for Dr. Osis's visit to the mill and the house.

The Old Grist Mill in Newlin's Mill Park, Concordville, across the road from a lovely park.

He arrived on a warm sunny Sunday, bringing Sylvia, a medium to assist him. Several friends, including some new ones from Parastudy, were invited to witness what might happen. Dr. Osis requested a tour of the house and mill so that he and Sylvia would be somewhat familiar with them. Even though it was not a working mill and was in deplorable condition, he wanted a glimpse inside.

Next chairs were placed in a semi-circle on the lawn. Dr. Osis and Sylvia took their seats in the open area in the middle. Claire and Bill were at the ends of the formation, while the guests filled in the other seats. Several brought materials to make notes since they'd been directed not to bring cameras.

Dr. Osis began by telling the group what he would try to do. He explained to Sylvia that he wanted her to relax, to place her hands in her lap, close her eyes, and let her body be at rest. He said that when he thought she was ready, he'd try to talk to the spirit of the woman who had been seen around the mill and would attempt to persuade her to talk to him through the medium. He would ask her to tell them why she was at the house. When he had learned all he could from the woman, he explained, he'd offer suggestions to help her find peace and rest.

Everyone sat very quietly as Dr. Osis began talking to Sylvia. As he gave her instructions for relaxing, several of the observers found themselves succumbing to his voice. After about fifteen minutes, Dr. Osis assured the group that Sylvia was sound asleep. He raised one of her arms. When he let go, it fell heavily into her lap. Then he began to call softly.

"Hello! Hello! I'm a friend who has come to visit you. Don't be afraid! Come, talk with me."

There was a brief silence. Dr. Osis repeated the invitation, using the same ideas, but different words. For awhile it seemed as though nothing was going to happen. Then Sylvia lifted her head and turned toward Dr. Osis. In a voice quite different from her own, and with a bit of a German accent, she began to speak.

"You're a friend? You won't beat me? You'll help me find my son?"

Questions and reassurances flew back and forth. Then Sylvia gave a big sigh and sank down in the chair. In a moment, she sat up as though ready to continue.

"Tell me your name," asked Dr. Osis.

"Sarah," she replied. He questioned her, gradually drawing out her story.

Sarah started by saying she became an orphan around the age of six or seven—she didn't recall exactly when. At that time she was sent to a workhouse—her earliest memory. She lived there until she was about twelve. One day a miller came to the workhouse looking for some household help. His wife had died, leaving him with two sons, and he needed someone to look after them and do the cooking and cleaning. Sarah was his choice because she was tall for her age and looked capable. It was a hard life for the young girl. When she prepared food the miller didn't like, he threw it on the floor and beat her. The sons fared no better. If they were not on time at meals, or were not in bed at the proper time, they too were beaten. When her chores in the house were finished, she had to help in the mill or tend the vegetable garden. In the evenings, she was expected to mend clothes or knit. Sarah was only sixteen when she married the miller. No one else played a role in her life. She had very little to say about her stepsons' lives.

In due time, a son was born—the third for the miller, but, of course, the first for Sarah. He was eight years younger than one stepbrother and ten years younger than the other. After the baby's birth, the miller became more cruel. He resented the time his wife spent with the child. How she loved the boy! Years passed. In 1861 the War Between the States began. The miller's two older sons immediately enlisted, glad of a reason to leave home. Occasionally they sent brief letters back telling of their experiences. Their younger brother poured over the missives and carried them about with him.

In the spring of 1863, the lad did something that irritated his father who immediately gave the boy the worst beating of his life and locked him in the mill for the entire night. The next morning the boy limped into the kitchen and begged his mother to go with him to the recruiting office so that he could join the army as his brothers had. That life had to be better than the one at home. He needed his mother to attest to his age. They both knew he was underage, but he was quite tall and could pass for seventeen if someone vouched for him. (Birth certificates were not in common use.) For several days Sarah and her son argued about the matter. During that time she also treated his wounds. Eventually Sarah conented.

The next Friday when Sarah drove the wagon to town for supplies, her son rode along. At the recruiting office, Sarah put her mark on the paper indicating her son was of legal age to enlist. Though he was barely fifteen, he soon received his orders and within a month left home. After a mere seven weeks in the army, he was killed.

When Sarah received the news of her son's death she nearly collapsed. Her husband had already punished her several times for lying about the boy's age. Gradually, as she mourned her son, her mind stopped functioning well. She began to reason that if she could find a paper, a note, anything that showed her son's true birth date or age, the army could be persuaded to send him home alive. She searched everywhere for evidence. After a few weeks of this, her husband became infuriated with her and gave her the worst beating she had ever received. Sarah reeled from the house, went to the rapidly moving mill stream and threw herself in, drowning almost instantly.

As Sarah told this story through Sylvia, guests were filled with the sadness of her emotion. Dr. Osis paused a few minutes in his questioning, then he continued. "Sarah, you told us a very sad story of your life. Think a minute. Wasn't there anything that ever made you happy? Try to remember."

There was stillness; then Sarah began to speak again.

"Yes," she replied, "there were two things that were good."

"Tell me about them," requested Dr. Osis gently.

"When I was a little girl living in the workhouse, one day our guardians took us to a park for a picnic. Some swings were there. I had my turn for a ride, and, oh, it was wonderful! The air rushed past me and blew my skirt above my head. My hair blew free. I didn't want to stop. Oh, it was wonderful! When I lived in the mill, I asked my husband to make a swing for the boys, but he wouldn't."

A smile lighted Sylvia's face as the voice quieted. Dr. Osis waited a short time, then he asked her what was the second happy experience she remembered.

Everyone listened intently for Sarah's story to continue. Sarah emitted a long sigh. Then she leaned back in her chair and began again.

"Fresh-baked bread! I have always loved the smell of fresh-baked bread. I love to make bread, to smell the yeast, to knead the dough—I'd really pound it when I was bothered. Then when it was time to bake, the wonderful aroma was everywhere. When my husband came in, the smell put him in a better mood. He always liked dinner, no matter what it was, baked beans, chicken, fried meat. But fresh-baked bread meant a quiet evening!"

Sylvia sighed as she settled back in her chair. Her whole face radiated a pleased, happy look. Then Dr. Osis began to talk to Sarah.

"Sarah," he began, "You've had a really bad time, but its over. You don't have to look for any papers. Your son is at peace and you should be too. Everything happened a long time ago. It's all over!

"Think about the happy things you've just described, a ride on a swing and fresh-baked bread. Remember them, then feel the peace those memories give you."

He continued to talk to Sarah for another half hour constantly reminding her to remember the happy events. He spoke more and more slowly until finally he stopped. Then, changing his tone of voice and moving a distance away from her, he requested Sylvia to waken, stand up and recover her usual composure. Fifteen or twenty minutes passed before she returned to a normal state. When this happened, the entire group stood and began talking. The whole experience had lasted almost three hours. Everyone suddenly realized what tension they had been under as they listened. It was as though they had been living the events of Sarah's life. The group besieged Dr. Osis with questions.

"Is she free now? Will she come back again? Where is she? What happens now?" These and others were on everyone's lips.

Dr. Osis quieted the group, then he began to speak.

"First of all, I don't know what Sarah will do—I don't know where she is. It will take time—it usually does—before Sarah understands everything we talked about. I hope she will send some sort of sign—that's why I emphasized her happy experiences. But I can't be sure. Every situation is different. We'll just have to wait and see.

Claire and Bill Brown said goodbye to their guests, promising to let them know if anything happened.

Weeks and then months passed. Claire and Bill were questioned about the lady by many of those who had been at the mill house with Dr. Osis. But the Browns had nothing to report. Then after four months, on a Friday afternoon, Claire and Bill placed excited phone calls to all the members of the group. Dr. Osis, of course, received the first one. He agreed that the Browns were right. Sarah had found peace.

Claire and Bill had been away from home nearly all day. They pulled into their driveway and climbed from the car. As they stepped on the porch, they heard a little girl laugh. But no one was there! Claire and Bill looked all around. Then they heard the laugh again and again.

"It's Sarah! On a swing! She's swinging! Listen!" Claire cried to Bill. The laugh sounded near where Claire was standing. Next it came from a few feet beyond. The next laugh rang out from the same place as the first. Bill and Claire just stood turning their heads as they followed the laugh. Gradually it faded and finally disappeared.

Claire turned to Bill with tears in her eyes and a smile on her face. "It's Sarah! She's all right!"

Bill nodded in agreement. He opened the kitchen door, took a step inside and stopped. Claire pushed past him, and she stopped too. The smell of fresh-baked bread permeated the air. The pair walked from room to room, the aroma filled the house. No matter where they went, that wonderful yeasty fragrance was there. After an excited hug, the couple ran for the phone. Dr. Osis, pleased to hear, agreed that the signs were positive. Sarah had at last found peace.

3

A Spirited Inn

Bart Johnson, owner of the General Wayne Inn on Montgomery Avenue in Merion, PA, was relaxing on a stool in the bar after a busy evening. It was late and everyone had left except two old friends of his. Miriam was the widow of the man who had played the piano in the dining room for twenty-nine years. Sophie, the other woman, had been employed there for a long time too. The three were chatting, sipping coffee at the Inn, and enjoying just being together for a little while. Suddenly the quiet was broken as a cannonball dropped from the ceiling with a heavy thud. It landed about fifteen feet in front of them in the dining room. The ball, larger than a tennis or baseball, was black with a rough surface. It began to roll slowly across the room towards them. Mr. Johnson rose and reached for the ball. As he did, it just disappeared. When he and his companions looked at the ceiling, they found no holes. Next they looked all around both the dining room and the bar but couldn't find the ball. Apparently it was one more unexplained event at the General Wayne Inn.

The General Wayne Inn on Montgomery Avenue, Merion, the home of the ghost of a hessian soldier (or two).

Built in 1704, the Inn has been an outstanding landmark ever since. At first it was known as the William Penn Inn, then Tunis Ordinary. (One way the word "ordinary" was used many years ago was to refer to a public house or a dining room serving all guests and customers the same fare. It reflects the British influence in the community.) The Inn next conducted business as Streepers' Tavern, then its name was changed to honor General

Anthony Wayne who had stayed there. Benjamin Franklin and George Washington also have been numbered among the important visitors. The building has been a post office, a coach stop, a bivouac for soldiers (particularly in Revolutionary days for Hessians), a central meeting place, and even today, a spot where vital questions of policies are discussed and decided. Not long ago it starred on the TV series *Unsolved Mysteries* in a segment that has been repeated frequently. The General Wayne is proud to be America's oldest restaurant.

Who or what haunts the place? Mr. Johnson is quick to say he doesn't know.

"Anyone that tells you he (or she) has shaken hands with a ghost, isn't telling the truth," he'll state with a smile, and a slight nod of his head. "But this I know—these things happen! Let me tell you!" And he relates another experience.

Managing the restaurant kept Bart Johnson away from home for long hours almost every day. He knew his wife regretted this, but that was the nature of the business. After much thought, Bart came up with an idea. He suggested his wife come with him and help. He knew she didn't want to work at the bar or in the dining room, and the kitchen was well staffed. However, he could use some assistance in the office. She agreed to take on some of the work. The first duty he asked her to assume was handling the credit card billings. The slips for the cards— American Express, Visa, Mastercard, etcetera were sorted. Then the amount billed to each company was added; a tally sheet placed on the top of the group. Finally the package was bundled and mailed to the company after the amount tallied was entered into a ledger.

There was an old adding machine on the office desk to use for the calculations. The first day Mrs. Johnson sorted the slips, and she added the figures in the first pile using the machine. She was puzzled by the total because it was so different from the figure she had reached mentally as she had worked through the pile, so she did it again. It was still wrong. Just roughly estimating it in her head as she went, she knew the total amount had to be around $1,000. But the machine showed a little over $400. Once more she added, saying the figures softly to herself. This time the total was over $10,000. Wrong again!

She called her husband into the office and explained the problem to him. He tried adding a small pile of slips, and again the machine was way off. He decided that the machine must have broken. Within a short time, Bart returned from a shopping trip with a new calculator. Placing the machine on his wife's desk, he plugged it into the socket.

Mrs. Johnson began again. Once more the total indicated on the machine was way off—and different from any of the others. While her husband had been shopping, Mrs. Johnson had added the slips manually. She attempted to add a set of figures a few more times but failed.

"This machine doesn't work either," she shouted to her husband. "Take it back!" She leaned in her chair wondering why neither machine would work properly. Then an idea developed.

She rose, walked across the office, opened the door, and stood aside. "Look, fellas!" she said to the open room, "You all have to leave! I have work to do! Come on! Out!" She continued to talk in this vein for several minutes. Then, closing the door and returning to her desk, she added the initial pile of slips once more. The total was correct. Mrs. Johnson quickly added the other piles, not only once, but twice—both times the totals were the same and were correct. Then she tried the old machine. It too worked accurately. Since then both machines have performed perfectly. The way she explains the problem is that the entities in the Inn were playing with the machines.

Who are these entities? One seems to be a Hessian soldier (or maybe there are two). The Hessians had been hired by the British and brought to America to fight the colonists. A Hessian soldier has been seen around the place fairly often. Some people claim he said his name was Max, but when a psychic visited the Inn, the soldier said his name was Wilhelm.

Years ago when Pennsylvania's liquor laws forbade the selling of liquor on Sunday, the Inn was always closed that day. It was the duty of a special porter to come on Sunday morning to clean the place after the Saturday night revelers had their fun.

One Sunday morning when Mr. Johnson came in sometime after ten o'clock to check on the work and complete some business, he found the cleaning unfinished, and no sign of the porter. Part of the main room had been carefully swept—the debris was brushed into piles half way cross the room. Chairs and tables on the clean side were all in their proper places ready for setting. But the rest of the room and the bar area were a mess.

Mr. Johnson shouted for the man several times but received no answer. He looked and called into the kitchen, the restrooms, the cellarway, but no one was around. Finally he picked up a phone and dialed the man's home number. To Bart's surprise, the porter answered the phone.

"Why are you home? Are you sick? Is something wrong? Your work isn't finished. Come back and clean up the rest of the place!" Mr. Johnson didn't sound pleased.

There was a pause, then came the response.

"I'm not coming back today. No, sir, no way. When I was about half done in the dining room, a noise made me look up. There in the far corner was standing a big soldier in one of those old fashioned uniforms. He was just looking at me. So I put down my broom, put on my coat, and walked out. I'm not coming back today."

The porter is not the only person to "see" the Hessian soldier. Somewhere through the years he acquired the name Max. However, even that changed after a visit from psychic Jean Quinn.

When Mrs. Jean Quinn, a prominent psychic, visited the Inn, she told Bart Johnson that she was aware of many spirits or entities in the place. She asked permission to visit the basement. That area is small compared to the rest of the inn. It has rough stone walls, and feels a bit damp. As Mr. Johnson watched, she began to run her hands up and down the walls. When he asked what she was doing, she said that she was looking for "cold spots" that would indicate a "presence" and requested permission to hold a "sitting" when the inn was quiet. Since the inn was closed on Mondays, a winter Monday night was chosen.

Jean brought several guests with her that night to observe. The Johnsons, including their two sons, were also present. It was a snowy evening which added to the aura of the place. Before commencing, Jean gave everyone three directions. First, loosen shoelaces, belts, anything that would be confining. Second, go to the bathroom. Once the sitting started, no one could leave the room. Third, have an overcoat or heavy sweater close by. If the sitting were to be successful the room would become cold. Then everyone went upstairs. There were chairs in the room around a table. Two recorders rested there. When everyone was seated, one of the younger Johnsons closed the two doors. Jean began with a prayer:

"Dear God, we are here to help anyone who needs us." At that the doors opened! Jean continued slowly:

"We welcome you! We're glad you're here! Tell us your name."

"Wilhelm" was the answer she received.

The Johnsons claim that they heard nothing and saw nothing save Jean seeming to talk to herself. She told the group that Wilhelm explained that he and his soldier companions had been stationed in the Inn. One particular winter evening, even though it was late, he chose to go for a walk. A short distance from the building, he was ambushed by a couple of colonials and killed. That was insult enough, but there was more. The next day a search party found his body and dragged it back to the Inn. A grave was dug nearby. However, before his body was dumped in, the commanding officer observed that the boots and uniform on the dead soldier were in good condition. The officer ordered that they be removed and replaced with his worn clothing. Then the officer dressed in the dead soldier's garments. Now, the voice of Wilhelm said, he was still looking for his clothes around the Inn.

Then other spirits or entities talked to the group through Jean. Two lady spirits, who said it was 1835 when asked to tell what year it was, described the Inn as they saw it—a busy place along a hard-packed dirt road. They told about many gatherings and groups who met at the Inn, and were eager to relate an incident involving a salesman. Traveling by horse and wagon, he stopped at the Inn to meet a prospective customer for his oriental rugs. In the early years of our nation, owning oriental rugs and/or venetian blinds were marks of distinction. The peddler stayed for a couple of days. When his prospect did not appear, the man went searching for him, leaving his rugs behind. He never returned. Though there is no record of what happened to the rugs, the ladies were still around in spirit believing they were blamed for stealing them.

Several other entities wanted an opportunity to be heard that night. One spoke in German so that revealed nothing. Another became hysterical and then faded away. A third one seemed to be a little boy searching for his mother. An Indian and a Black spoke briefly, but their reasons for staying around were unclear. Altogether it was an amazing session, but the most amusing revelation came from Wilhelm. He reported that he could drink only one thing in this strange country—tea. He felt the beer was

too weak and mild, the whiskies raw and the wines sour. But
fresh-brewed tea could be as strong as the drinker wished.
Altogether it was quite an evening.

However, that evening was not the end of Wilhelm. In the 1970s
Mr. Johnson came in contact with a man from Oliphant,
Pennsylvania, a small town in the northeastern part of the state.
The man, aged 37, was in a contracting business. On a Saturday
night the gentleman was awakened from his sleep by a Hessian
soldier sitting on his bed. The ghostly figure stated that he was
from the General Wayne Inn and that he needed help. While he
was stationed at the Inn, some Colonials had sneaked in through
openings in the wall and killed him. Because the weather was
bad, the Colonials dug a hole in the thick walls and buried his
body. He still wanted a proper burial. Apparently the entity
wakened his host several times. Finally the man from Oliphant
came to the Inn, reported his experience, and asked permission
to try to locate the Hessian's bones. Reluctantly, Mr. Johnson
gave his consent for some exploration. Digging began in one
basement wall, and precautions were taken not to damage the
Inn. When the excavations began to stretch under the present
parking lot, floors became a bit shaky and Mr. Johnson called a
halt. Debris was hauled to the surface in buckets. Sure enough,
when the material was shifted, bone fragments were found. Mr.
Johnson won't say what happened to the bones, but he does
report he had to hire someone to repair the damage the digging
created. The man in Oliphant had no more spirit visitors.

However the Hessian (or Hessians) still appear. A Lower Merion
business group of men held a Christmas party at the General
Wayne in December, 1990. It seemed to be a success. Three

months later a man from New York visited the Inn again and talked to Mr. Johnson. He remarked on the unique touch at the party and how much he enjoyed it.

"What unique touch? Mr. Johnson wanted to know.

"Why the Hessian soldier!" the man replied. "He walked all around, smiled and mingled with groups then moved on. We all thought that was a clever touch in this old place!"

Mr. Johnson knew nothing about the soldier, had not seen him, nor hired anyone to act the role. Was Max/Wilhelm back? It would seem so.

However, some of the bizarre events have nothing to do with Hessians, however many there are.

One Friday evening, after all the visitors were gone, the staff quickly put the main dining room and bar area in order and set the tables for a wedding luncheon to be held at noon the next day. When they left together, each place setting was in order, napkins standing erect and glasses ready for filling. When Mr. Johnson unlocked the door the next morning about 9:30, every single napkin had been unfolded and tossed on the floor.

Another incident shows the strange way the entities behave. In Pennsylvania, liquor could not be sold on election day until evening except in private clubs. On one particular election day, the staff of the Inn was to report in late afternoon to prepare for the evening trade. As Mr. Johnson entered the bar area, his eyes picked up a glint from the cash register drawer. It was customary to remove all the money at night and to leave the drawer partially open. As he looked again, the drawer seemed to have mirrors in the various compartments. Mr. Johnson pulled open the drawer and discovered it was full of water. What a job to empty that! And when he did, he discovered water had seeped through and damaged the machine so that it wouldn't work. Then the bartenders and Mr. Johnson discovered the speed tray along the bar was full of water. Further checking revealed 32 wine carafes in the overhead racks were also full of water. No explanation has ever been found.

If you visit the General Wayne for luncheon, or for dinner, you'll be served a lovely meal. Perhaps you'll feel, or sense, an unseen guest. Or you may hear about one of the times when all 1,200 glasses in the cases over the bar began to shake, touching and chiming against each other without breaking. That went on for four to five minutes. It happened again the next day, and the next, for a month, then stopped. A month later, the shaking was repeated for four weeks. Who knows when it will happen again.

If you drive, it is recommended that you permit the valet service to handle your car. A brand new car, a very elegant one, was driven to the Inn one busy Saturday night, but its owner refused to leave it with the valet. The owner parked the car himself and pocketed the keys. Part way through his dinner, the guest was asked to attend to his car. The lights were on, the motor was running, the windshield wiper was rapidly waving, the stereo was blaring, and the horn was sounding! It was a very disgruntled owner who reluctantly yielded his keys to the valet after silencing his automobile. But at the General Wayne anything can be expected.

4

Open Doors

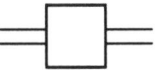

M any people believe that ghosts, spirits, or entities are found only in old buildings—houses, inns, churches. That's primarily because old places have been around long enough to have acquired a reputation for whatever seems to be occurring. However, in a community in New Jersey, not far from the Benjamin Franklin Bridge, a contractor built three houses on lots next to each other. The house on the left as you face them from the street and middle house are mirrors of each other. The right hand one is exactly like the one on the left. All three are modified two-story, Cape Cod types. Each is part yellow brick and part vinyl siding. The front doors are soft yellow wood with small windows. Shutters define the three front windows on the first floor. The builder planted low shrubbery around the foundations, then put the houses on the market. Each sold quickly. The families who purchased the one on the left and the center one were pleased with their selections, and found only minor problems to be remedied. The house on the right, however, has caused severe headaches to many people.

Three houses in New Jersey. Two are lovely homes, but the third was in the wrong place and had to be changed.

On the day the first owners—parents of twin three-year-old daughters—moved into it, the place was in the usual "first moved-in muddle". At bedtime, the new owner, Henry, locked the front and back doors, turned off lights as he carefully slipped past boxes and went upstairs.

The next morning when the family came downstairs, the front door was wide open. Henry knew he had locked it before retiring. He closed the door, turned the lock, then shook the door hard. It didn't seem at all loose. He rationalized that maybe he had been more tired than he realized the night before and hadn't quite turned the lock. The second night, at bedtime, he carefully checked the lock—it was good and tight. But the next morning, the door was wide open again. No one had been downstairs; no one else should even have a key. The third night, after locking the door, Henry pushed a chair against it. In the morning the chair was pushed aside and the door was open. Henry phoned the builder and complained.

By evening, a new lock had been placed on the door. At bedtime Henry ascertained that the door was secure, then he retired. His wife, Anita, went downstairs first the next day. It was the weekend.

"Henry!", she called in an upset tone, "come down here!"

Half asleep, Henry staggered down the steps and turned toward the door. It was wide open as was the window next to it. Rain was blowing in through both. Henry slammed the door shut as Anita tugged at the window. It took both of them to pull it down and turn the lock. An irate and damp Henry phoned the builder and demanded that something be done to the door immediately.

Within an hour, the builder and an assistant arrived, giving Henry time to dress and calm himself a bit. After hanging canvas to keep out the rain, the workmen carefully removed the door from its hinges. Another new lock was installed, the hinges and all the side fittings were checked. Everything seemed fine as the door was carefully set in place. All the windows were checked even though only one had been open. The next morning, everything was closed and locked just as Henry and Anita left them before going to bed.

Monday morning was quite different. The front door and all

three windows were wide open! Once more Henry reached for the phone.

This time when the builder arrived, Henry shouted that he and his family would move out and that he wanted his money returned unless the problem was corrected immediately. The builder left, only to return an hour later with several workmen. They toiled all day rebuilding the door, its frame, and the windows. But Tuesday morning everything was open again.

Henry and family moved out. Then the builder took off the entire lower front of the house and reconstructed it, taking several weeks to complete the work as carefully as possible. Again the house was placed on the market and sold fairly quickly. The new owners were not told of the problem the former ones had experienced, but the same thing happened to them. They managed to stay almost three weeks before they left. Meanwhile nothing at all happened to the other two homes.

A third family bought the now "open house" as the builder called it. He had employed several consultants and had tried their suggestions for redoing the front of the house. He even relocated the front door and the windows. The first night the new family stayed in the house all went well, but the second morning when they went downstairs, the place was a shambles. The door was open, all the window sashes had been removed and were broken on the floor. Strangely the three members of the family heard nothing. It didn't take very many days with similar mornings to persuade them to leave.

For several months, the house sat vacant with its front door and windows boarded. One afternoon, the builder returned with several people and some folding chairs. Removing the boards from the doorway, he led the group inside. Prior to their arrival he had told them about his problem. One of his guests was a "sensitive," a person who tries to sense or feel what happened at a particular place. The others were his friends. The "sensitive" gentleman walked all around the house, upstairs and down. Sitting on one of the chairs that had been brought inside, he talked with the group, and he explained that he felt a great sadness come over him—he wasn't sure why. He speculated that someone may have been murdered on the spot where the house was built. Or, he said, it may have been the scene of an Indian slaughter. For about half an hour he speculated about what tragedy had occurred there, but refused to pinpoint one. He felt quite certain that a man was the person who died there and that his spirit resented being trapped inside the house. The builder didn't accept the explanation but offered no other.

About a year later, the house was offered for sale again, with the same disastrous results. Finally, the builder just tore it down and sold the lot. The new owner built a house a short distance further back on the lot. This place has never had a problem.

5

Beechwood's Clara

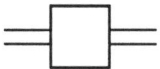

My house in Havertown was built as an inn in 1757. Deep springs in the rear area of the grounds were the reason the site was chosen. They still give nine gallons of water every half hour of every day. The house remained an inn until the early 1800s serving local mill workers and residents at its bar and housing travelers. Then it became a farm house, and the land was primarily used for breeding, raising and selling horses.

In the early 1900s, when the rail line west from the Upper Darby area opened, an amusement park was built by the Beechwood-Brookline station to attract riders. This house became a club house. People rented boats to use on the lake. A family or young lovers enjoyed picnic tables and fireplaces for a modest sum. Shortly after my family moved in, we met two elderly brothers who asked to visit our rear garden. Telling us how they had "sparked their wives" there, they described the area as it looked then when the park was in operation in 1909.

The park and the clubhouse closed in 1909. For a few years, the house stood empty. Then a young engineer bought it, repaired it, and brought his bride there. Our family purchased it from that family's daughter after her mother's death. Her father had died earlier.

We moved in as a large family—two parents, three grandparents, four children, one foster child, and a great assortment of pets. The twenty-room house was exactly what we needed. There was plenty of space for everyone.

Now a family home, this was an Inn, and a farm house where a troublesome ghost no longer roams.

Before long the two grandmothers, who had always been friendly, began to argue. Each insisted she saw a lady in the living room, the music room, a hallway, or a sitting room. Both were upset because each thought the other had a guest visiting and didn't want to share the friendship. Grandfather Hoffman just assumed it was a neighbor who wandered in. One day Beth, our daughter, ran upstairs to give Grandmother Parkinson a library book. Returning to the first floor, she asked me if the lady by the window at the head of the stairs was the one her grandmothers argued about. I hastened upstairs, but could not find a visitor anywhere in the hall, in any bedroom, or sitting room. Beth's description of a stiff-backed lady in a long dress matched that which the grandmothers gave.

Lloyd, our six-year old, began to sleep with a pillow over his head.

"A lady comes and looks at me! I don't like her" he insisted when questioned. After suggesting and having rejected all sorts of possibilities that might create the illusion of a woman's figure, we told him to ask the strange woman what she wanted. A few evenings later, when I checked on him before I retired, his head was on top of the pillow. In the morning when waking Lloyd for school, I asked him what caused the change. He explained that, gathering his courage, he talked to the lady who told him she liked boys and would watch over him. So my son talked to imaginary old ladies!

We all became aware of a strange sound that occurred everywhere in the house. The most frequent places were the bookcase corner of the living room, and in the upstairs hall by the first window. It sounded like someone gasping and gulping for breath, like a person with asthma. We couldn't detect any logical explanation for it. Sometimes it would go on for three or four minutes. On other occasions, it was just a moment or two. At first we blamed the children for creating the noise but could find no proof. When we heard it in the same room we were in, we had a very uneasy feeling. Eventually even the youngsters were disconcerted by it.

Something else began to annoy them too. Except for six-year- old Lloyd, each child was scheduled a time to use the music room for practice. The sliding doors were to be closed for both privacy and quiet. However, each youngster in turn complained that the room was cold, even though the thermometer registered 74 degrees, and there was a fire burning in the hearth. They also said they felt someone was watching them. Terry, our middle son, was practicing his mellophone one day when the platform rocker began to move. No one was in it that he could see. That practice session ended fast!

Several times visitors started to sit in that chair then rose quickly before they were quite seated. "I felt as though I were sitting on someone's lap" one guest said while selecting a different seat. Another friend saw a lady rocking and suggested we not go in the room and bother her. On a damp November Sunday, two friends visited who lived in Puerto Rico. They were staying with their family in New Jerey and came to spend an afternoon with me. As it began to darken outside, I invited them to stay for supper. Dorothy remained in the living room while Shirley went to the kitchen and dining room with me. I should note that by now Grandfather Hoffman had died; Grandmother Hoffman was in a nursing home; and on this weekend, Grandmother Parkinson was visitng my brother 400 miles away. When we were almost ready to sit down to eat, Dorothy entered the dining room and counted places. Seeing a questioning look on her face, I asked her what was wrong.

"There aren't enough places" she replied. "I counted children, guests, family, and you're one short."

"I don't think so," I answered then named someone for each seat.

"Well, isn't your mother coming?"

"My mother! Why do you ask?"

"Isn't your mother coming to the table or do you take her a tray? If so, I can do that for you" Dorothy answered.

"Where is she now?" I asked trying to sound casual. I realized Dorothy really thought she saw my mother—or at least an older woman.

"She's sitting in the rocking chair beside the organ in the room beyond the hall."

I hurried to the music room. The chair was rocking slowly, but I saw no one. I told Dorothy that Mother didn't want to eat yet— she would have something later. I knew if I told Dorothy she had seen a "ghost" lady she would have returned to New Jersey so fast we couldn't have caught her.

Several other people had similar experiences with the chair, we decided not to tell them what we thought they were seeing. Finally we just pushed the chair into a corner and ignored it. It could rock whenever it wished!

The cold that the children complained of in the music room made itself felt periodically in various spots all over the house. Sometimes people sitting on the sofa in the living room, even with a good blaze in the fireplace, would feel a very cold spot develop between them. No window or door could create that kind of a draft. Or as we walked down a hallway, we sometimes felt as though we'd past an open refrigerator. Often we felt someone watching us. The room might be empty, but we were uneasy. Did we all have overactive imaginations?

When knives and scissors began to disappear that was almost too much! Naturally the children were blamed, but they denied taking them. Grandmother Parkinson's large scissors disappeared from their hook on her loom while every one was away on a vacation trip. My paring and chopping knives vanished from the kitchen regularly and had to be replaced. A search of the boys' rooms did not uncover them, nor could we find evidence of carving or whittling.

On the first day of spring vacation after this started, I decided to thoroughly clean the dining room with my housekeeper's help. Pat tackled the windows while I emptied the buffet drawers, placed fresh liners, and arranged the contents in good order. When the front doorbell rang, I placed the roll of lining paper and the pair of new scissors I had purchased the night before on top of the buffet. Then going to the front hall, I greeted the delivery man, signed for the package, and returned to the dining room. Pat, who was standing by the French doors at the end of the room, was visibly upset.

"Why did you throw those scissors? They scared me, and they could have hurt me!" she said accusingly. I glanced at the top of the buffet. No scissors. Looking where Pat was pointing, I saw them, points embedded in the rug, on the far side of the table. Even if I had dropped them, they wouldn't have gone that far. Pat secured her sweater and purse, asked for her wages, and left muttering about too many strange things in the house. We had to find a new housekeeper.

Did you ever watch a cat rub itself around someone's ankles, look up purring and enjoy a patting? That's fine when you can see the person doing the caressing but a little strange when you can see no one. Obviously the cat can! Our cats did this regularly. They saw someone who we didn't and enjoyed a good fondling.

Footsteps pacing the halls all night; doors that opened by themselves; housekeepers that quit after a few days, saying the place was "creepy;" chairs that were continually overturned these and other experiences made us look into the literature of ghosts.

We questioned neighbors who told us "everyone knew that the house was haunted." We found there were several groups in the Philadelphia area who were knowledgeable on the subject and didn't think we were fools. We talked at length with them and read much material they gave us. Many of these people visited the house and became good friends. One person suggested that when we heard the breathing, or the footsteps, or felt the cold, we should tell the entity to go away, using a woman's name since all the sightings apparently were of a woman. We recorded the names we used. One evening as my husband and I heard the breathing moving across the living room, we spoke to it: "Are you Clara? Please go away! That will tell us now who you are." The breathing stopped in mid gasp.

Shortly afterwards, our search of records indicated that a Clarinda Johnson had lived in the house for almost 25 years. Was she the source of our problem? In the summer of 1961, we found more evidence that someone or something was busy. Our eldest son underwent surgery that fused several vertebrae and confined him to bed for the entire summer. He used a bedroom on the first floor so we could care for him, and he would be near everyone. Before he entered the hospital, he and I put his top floor room in order and locked the door. I kept one key and locked the other in a strong box. The night after his surgery, my husband and I heard his desk chair scrape across the floor. When we unlocked the door, we found the whole room upset—the bed crumpled, a waste basket upset, books spilled, and, of course, the desk chair pulled into the middle of the room. This happened several times during the summer while our son was confined in a large body cast to the room on the first floor.

Arthur Ford, one of America's outstanding psychics, came to Philadelphia to lecture to the Parapsychology Society of Greater Philadelphia. After the lecture, he appeared on a talk show on WCAU with the late Alan Scott to discuss hauntings. An officer of the organization Ford addressed invited my husband and me to attend the lecture and to meet Ford. Since we had learned

quite a bit about Ford and had studied his book, *Nothing So
Strange,* we eagerly accepted the invitation. Ford had worked
with such people as Conan Doyle and Sir Oliver Lodge and was
well known for his work with hauntings and ghosts. Our
excitement increased when I was invited to join Mr. Ford for
the radio show to talk about what we had been experiencing.
Since our home is near WCAU, we asked Mr. Ford and his
friends to our home for refreshments and relaxation after the
lecture and before the talk show. We agreed we would not tell
him that this was the house that would be discussed later on
the show.

That special summer evening we attended the lecture in
Glenside then hastened home to greet our guests, about a dozen,
some of whom we already knew because of the research we had
been doing. They included The Reverend William Rauscher, an
Episcopalian priest from New Jersey, The Reverend Canon
Robert J. Lewis, Mrs. Beatrice Chegg, a hypnotist from
Huntington Valley, Mr. Melvin Sutley formerly of Wills Eye
Hospital and Richard Van Meter, an engineer. After half an hour,
Mr. Ford excused himself to freshen for the broadcast. When he
returned to the dining room he announced, "I just met your
friend Clara in the upstairs hall. She was pointing out the window
to the pond where the horses and cattle were watered when this
was a farm. Is the pond still there?"

We just looked at him. He had arrived after dark, driven by Mr.
Rauscher. He could not possibly have seen much of the grounds
since the house is only 20 feet from the street with most of the
two acres of land in the back. I described our small pond.

"No," he insisted, "it was like a lake." He couldn't see it all because of the trees. I immediately described the lake that used to be there.

"But she drowned!" Mr. Ford stated. "She faded from the hall and I saw her pulled into the water. Her skirts were very heavy."

The group in the dining room was varied in their reactions. Those who had experienced Clara in some way nodded—they weren't surprised that Mr. Ford had met her. And others, who thought the whole thing was imagined, were amazed. We had to leave for the studios at this point. During the program, Mr. Alan Scott led the discussion of the whole situation with Mr. Ford, Mr. Sutley, and me. I received some suggestions for learning more about Clara and other spirits. Mr. Ford called the house a waystation for many spirits—most of them visitors at the Inn, but a few former residents. But he assured me that Clara was the only troublesome spirit.

We renewed our search for deeds and other information about our home and Beechwood. We scoured old newspaper files, feeling that a drowning would be newsworthy. Finally we located a newspaper story stating that a Jane Johnson drowned in Beechwood. It also indicated that Jane was Clara's cousin. She too lived in this house. Clara apparently saw Jane drown. Arthur Ford did not realize the woman he met in the hall and the woman he saw drowning were not the same woman.

Dr. Carrol Nash of St. Joseph's University arranged for Mrs. Eileen Garrett to visit us to suggest ways to put our spirit at peace. Mrs. Garrett, a world-famous Irish medium, helped to develop the

International Parapsychological Foundation. When she arrived, she was accompanied by Martin Ebon, (well known for his own research), two ministerial students from Union Theological Seminary in New York, and a camera crew. For several hours Mrs. Garrett walked around the house both inside and out. She sat in the rocking chair and went into a trance—a deep sleep so that Clara could speak through her. Clara's story was a sad one.

As a young widow, Clara had moved to the house in Beechwood from Vermont with two sons, a cousin, and a niece. Horses were the love of her life. She bred them, raised them, and traded them. She said she could "out deal, out trade, and out smart any man in the county." It seems that Clara was very unethical in her dealings. She had virtually no friends, and she ordered her relatives around like they were servants. The hired hands disliked her too. Although she wanted love and respect, she repelled people by her actions. She lost one of her sons when he was very young; the other was killed in a barroom brawl. Her cousin's death embittered her more. One day she fell down a flight of steps severely injuring her head. Fearing doctors, saying they would cut her head where the injury was, she refused medical treatment. Eventually she took to her bed where she succumbed from her injuries.

Mrs. Garrett told us we must pray for Clara's peace; must stop thinking of her as a disagreeable person, even though she was, and try to send her love and good thoughts. If we had friends willing to help, that would be good too. We should tell Clara (when we sensed she was around), that while we were concerned for her, she should leave the house—it was ours now, not hers. Mrs. Garrett gave us many suggestions but stressed that our attitude was important.

At first our family felt foolish talking to empty space. We sat with friends, or by ourselves, in the music room, primarily asking for guidance, for help, and for peace. We learned to look forward to the quiet times of meditation and prayer. Gradually the house became more comfortable—cold spots didn't appear so often, footsteps diminished, the breathing sounds faded.

There was one evening when four friends were in the music room with us that we all felt that the prayers and positive suggestions might not be enough. The room was suddenly very icy. One window rattled as though someone was banging it. There was no wind so it couldn't have been that. Gradually the sound faded and the room warmed. As we talked about the experience over tea, one person insisted she hadn't felt or heard anything, even when we joined in group prayer. We couldn't understand that.

A little more than a year later we had another meeting with Mr. Ford, who by this time had moved to Philadelphia. He assured us, through Fletcher, his spirit guide, that Clara had indeed found peace. All of this sounds easy to do, but it really wasn't. Doubts, questions, and occasionally even sadness besieged us. But we still felt good about what we were doing. We wanted to enjoy our home without annoyance. We haven't missed Clara— although the children did for a time. Unmade beds, towels on the bathroom floor, empty milk bottles in the refrigerator, unwashed dishes all were blamed on her. The children began to think every family should have a resident ghost. What an excuse!

Yes, there are some other entities that come and go around the place. A sailor with a peg leg occasionally startles someone. One youngster who saw him wanted to know why he had a stick tied to his leg. We don't see peg legs any more except in the old movies.

Shadows move across the floor when there is nothing to create them. Seasonal "travelers" seem to stop by but never stay.

Our cats occasionally see someone, but we don't worry about that. Visitors like to touch the old carriage stone out front for good luck. Special guests are shown a paper booklet we found behind a baseboard during a construction project. It has Clara's name in it—a solid connection with our ghost.

6

Historical Hauntings

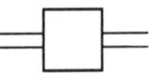

The Liberty Bell, Independence Hall, the Betsy Ross House—these are the places that come to most people's minds first when Philadelphia is mentioned. In the same historic area there are other outstanding landmarks, including Christ Church with Benjamin Franklin's grave close by, the First and Second National Banks, and Carpenters' Hall. Visitors may spend all day in the area and still not see everything.

Although all of these places have an aura of both history and mystery about them, Carpenters' Hall seems to have its own resident ghost as well as its own unique place in American history.

Designed by Robert Smith in 1770 and built by members of the Carpenter's Company, Carpenters' Hall sits back from Chestnut Street near the Visitor's Center. The brick building contains three floors and a basement. On the first floor there is an entrance hall across the front of the building. Directly behind that is a large meeting room. Chairs there indicate where the master carpenters and (in 1774) the First Continental Congress met. It was in this room during the congressional meetings that Patrick Henry of Virginia gave one of his oft quoted speeches:

"The distinction between Virginians, Pennsylvanians, New Yorkers, and New Englanders are no more. I am not a Virginian but an American."

A small gift and souvenir shop now occupies the southeast corner. On the second floor on the right is a library which includes some of Franklin's books—his library was moved here in 1774. On the left side of the floor is the caretaker's apartment. Above, on the third floor are a few very small rooms which in early years were rented to members of the Carpenter's Company. Some are empty and some are used for storage. The basement area contains several small rooms which through the years have served as bank vaults and most recently have contained laundry facilities. Outside, the grounds on the side and rear are nicely landscaped. A passerby on Chestnut Street could easily miss the building. It is still owned by the Carpenter's Company who recently restored much of its exterior.

As I mentioned before, the First Continental Congress, to which all the American colonies except Georgia sent representatives, met here in 1774. This Congress set the stage for others which moved to the nearby State House—Independence Hall. This included the Second Continental Congress, which signed the Declaration of Independence, and later the Constitutional Convention.

*A side view of Carpenters' Hall, off Chestnut Street
in the historic area of Philadelphia, scene of an early robbery.*

Following the Revolution and the establishment of a new nation,
the first floor and basement area were rented to the Bank of
Pennsylvania. The rooms on the top floor continued to be
rented, as they always had been, to members of the Company
who were unmarried or who didn't have a home. Since the space

in each room was small, the furniture was limited to
necessities—a bed, chair, small chest, clothes rack, and little if
anything else. On September 1, 1798, two men arrived at the bank
on horseback shortly after closing time. Their clothes and their
wigs were dirty and disheveled. Using a key, they entered the
bank and held up the cashier who had been closing out the day's
receipts. One of the men brandished a gun.

Since the money had just been counted, but not yet stored in
the vault, the exact amount of $162,821.16 was known and
recorded. Toting the bags containing the money, the thieves
mounted their horses and rode off. The police from the Walnut
Street station were summoned. After listening to the description
of what happened and asking questions, they arrested Pat
Lyon, a locksmith on Walnut Street. He had just recently put a
new lock on the front door, had provided keys for the men
who lived there and for the bank, and still had a key. Even
though he protested his innocence, Pat was arrested and jailed
for masterminding the theft.

A week later, two men came into the bank to open an account
with money they claimed they found. The amount was
$162,821.16. One of the men was Isaac Davis, a house builder who
lived a short distance away and was a member of the Carpenter's
Company. With him was Tom Cunningham who lived in one of
the small rooms on the third floor and had one of the new keys to
the building. Although he too was a carpenter, his name does not
appear in the records as a member of the Company.

Police were again summoned and these two were accused of
working for Lyon, and they were arrested. No one is sure why,

but Davis and Cunningham left the jail after a few days, while Lyon languished there. Davis was dismissed from the Company—his name on the membership roster is marked with an X. Cunningham returned to his room ill with yellow fever which he caught in prison. Raging with fever, he died within a week. Meanwhile Lyon remained in prison for two more months trying to prove his innocence. When he finally was successful, he was released and paid $10,000.00 in reparation for his false arrest.

It was some time after Cunningham's death that the ghostly sounds began on the third floor. Other residents up there vowed they heard Tom, or someone like him stomping in heavy boots up and down the hallway. Occasionally the footsteps went partway down the stairs. Banging noises came from Tom's former room. There is no record to indicate how long rooms were rented up there or who rented them.

In 1857, just before the Civil War broke out (1861) the Hall was dedicated as a public shrine and opened to the public by the Carpenter's Company. The group has provided caretakers for it. James and Hazelle O'Connor were employed in that capacity in 1960 and moved into the second floor apartment. They were just beginning to enjoy living in the historic building and were becoming familiar with all its rooms and furnishings when something disturbing happened.

They had retired for the night and had just fallen asleep when they were awakened by the sound of footsteps stomping overhead. Since no one else was supposed to be in the building, James reached for the phone and called the police. Two officers were dispatched to the Hall. Pulling on robes,

James and Hazelle very quietly opened a window in the front room of the apartment and threw the key to the main door to the officers standing below. The men came in, climbed quietly up the stairs to the second floor then stopped. The sounds on the third floor ceased abruptly. With one hand on a gun and a flashlight in the other, the officers continued their climb. Hazelle and Jim could hear the men—their footsteps were not as fast-moving or as heavy as the others. But then the couple realized that the first ones—the footsteps that had wakened them had stopped. Shortly after the officers returned to the second floor and entered the apartment at Hazelle's invitation.

"Nobody up there! Nobody's been there—there are no foot prints in the dust!"

"But we heard them! They woke us up!" insisted both O'Connors. The argument went back and forth.

"You'd better do something about the smell! It's really bad!" remarked one of the patrolmen while writing his report. "May be a dead animal up there. That stench will keep anyone out! Don't worry about the noise too much. Other people who've lived here have complained about the sounds up there. But there's never anyone around."

After drinking some coffee, the patrolmen left. For Hazelle and James, sleep was ruined. As they compared reactions to the night's events, they decided to look upstairs themselves.

Carefully they opened the apartment door and went into the hall. It was still lighted from the earlier visit. They began to climb the stairs to the third floor but by the time they were half way up, the horrible smell was so nauseating that Hazelle backed down the steps quickly and ran into their rooms. James followed, slamming the apartment door closed.

The next morning when they went into the second floor hall, the odor was gone. Both O'Connors searched the top floor. Everything was undisturbed except for the footprints of the patrolmen in the dust. It was a puzzle.

A few nights later the footsteps and banging came again. Turning on a light beside the bed, James noted the time was 2:10 a.m. When he opened the apartment door a little, the odor greeted him. Hazel turned the radio on high volume as they sat wondering and waiting for the noise to stop. It seemed to last a long time, but actually it was only about 20 minutes. Again, the couple had difficulty going back to sleep. After a third occurrence, Hazelle was ready to move out but her husband refused.

As they realized that nothing really hurt them, the O'Connors developed a routine. In the early evening they would fill a bottle with drinking water from the cooler in the outer hall. That way they didn't even have to open the door for that. At bedtime they would set the radio or TV in the front room on high volume then close the bedroom door. That masked most of the noise. A couple of psychics were invited to visit the third floor. They didn't even hear the noise, but they visited during the day, not at night. Just as they were ready to leave, one of the psychics pushed open the door to the last room. Something seemed to rush out nearly knocking the pair to the floor. The odor, so familiar to Hazelle who had accompanied them, filled the area. However, no one saw anything—they only felt and smelled it.

The basement area seemed to have unseen visitors too. When the O'Connors' son, an explorer, came to visit, he was given a bed in a small basement room. Within fifteen minutes of entering the room, he returned to the upstairs apartment dragging a sleeping bag with him and reported to his parents that he felt a presence, even though he couldn't see it, and it made him most uncomfortable. Only then did they inform him of their experiences.

Hazelle disliked climbing and descending the narrow winding steps to the basement with a full laundry basket when she was doing the family wash. She persuaded one of the guards to put a chair near the appliances so that she could sit and read, or sew, or even daydream if she wished. The second day she went down, the chair fell over as she passed it. She righted it and placed her laundry basket on the seat. The chair fell over again. Hurrying upstairs, she picked up a small dog she'd recently acquired and took him back down with her. James was at his office so she couldn't reach him. As soon as she put the animal on the floor, his ears and head went down, his tail curled between his legs, and (issuing low growls) he backed out of the room and flew up the steps. Hazelle decided the dog had the right idea, and she sprinted after him. The wash could wait until another day when one of the guards could accompany her.

Guests of the O'Connors frequently sensed a heaviness in the air when they visited. One described it as "the way air feels just before a heavy thunderstorm breaks." What causes this? Is the presence in the basement the same as the one that makes the footsteps? Or is there more than one? If you talk with Hazelle "off the record," she suggests that the ghost of Tom Cunningham, whose body succumbed to yellow fever, is the presence she and her husband hear at night. She won't venture a guess about the basement.

In 1974, an event occurred that provided even more evidence that Carpenters' Hall was home to ghosts. That year, Governor Milton Shapp hosted a meeting of the Governors' Conference, in the Hall to observe the hundredth anniversary of the First Continental Congress. It was a busy, exciting day with dignitaries all over the building. As the O'Connors prepared to retire, they both wished for a quiet night. It was not to be. The stillness was broken with sounds of shouting and quarreling coming from just below them. The couple knew no one could be down there. They had made the final check themselves, locking the front door, and then giving it a hard tug. Although they listened carefully to the argument coming from downstairs, they couldn't make out the words. They did hear several different voices. Occasionally a chair scraped on the floor. It seemed as though the noise went on a long time, but, actually, it wasn't more than five or six minutes. The O'Connors knew what to do. They turned up the radio and went to bed.

The next morning, before the regular working staff arrived, Hazelle and James went downstairs to check the room. Every chair was as they had left it—in the semicircle. They detected the smell of tobacco but found no cigarette stubs, no pipe tobacco ashes, no burned matches. As they discussed what they had heard the night before, the O'Connors could reach only one conclusion. Some of the revolutionary firebrands of 1774 had come back so they, too, could mark the anniversary.

The O'Connors never heard the voices below their apartment again. Only the basement and top floor visitors seem to stay. Hazelle says they're spirits enough for any house.

7

A Life Saving Ghost

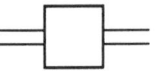

On a lovely street in Lansdowne is a large, old twin house. The home on the right as you face the building has a ghost who, according to tenants who lived there in the 1970s, saved a man's life. Many ghosts or spirits are credited with scaring people nearly to death, but this one did quite the opposite.

Charles, Maria, and their young daughter, Olivia, rented the home while Charles was engaged in graduate study in Philadelphia. His wife was busy caring for their almost five-year-old daughter. Maria drove in a carpool for a nursery/ kindergarten and participated in other community activities. The first few weeks of the family's stay in the house were comfortable and uneventful.

One evening as Maria was preparing dinner, she heard her daughter, who was playing in the livingroom, talking to someone. Olivia had not been a child who talked to herself, but Maria clearly heard her speaking. Walking into the living room, Maria looked all around, then saw the child in the entrance hall looking up the stairs. As her mother watched, Olivia held up her arms as if to catch something.

"Throw it! Throw it!" Olivia called as she looked up the steps toward the second floor. Maria moved into the hall and looked up the steps too. She saw no one.

"Who are you talking to?" she asked her daughter.

"Her," was the reply, "she won't give my pillow back!" Olivia pointed up the stairs. Just short of the second floor was a small landing. If you climbed the stairs and turned to the right on the landing, a few steps would bring you to the front hall. Or if you went across the landing toward the rear of the house and stepped up a few stairs, you would reach the back hall and two rooms in the rear of the house. Maria turned so she could see in both directions, but no one was there.

"Make her give me my pillow, Mommy," Olivia cried. "It's mine." Maria moved toward her daughter as Olivia began to mount the steps. As quickly as she started, she stopped and turned toward her mother, a puzzled look on her face.

"Where did she go, Mommy? Where's the girl with my pillow?" she asked.

"What girl?" her mother questioned. "There's no girl here! You just imagined it. Maybe the living room light made shadows that seemed like a girl!"

But Olivia insisted she saw a girl standing part way up the stairs and holding the special pillow that Olivia hugged when she went to bed. Taking Olivia's hand, Maria led her to the steps and started to climb while she soothed her daughter with calming words. She stopped suddenly as she neared the landing and pulled Olivia's hand so strongly the child almost fell. As her eyes came even with the landing, she saw Olivia's pillow lying there. It was a small, round off white pillow about fourteen inches in diameter with a bunny face embroidered on it. Olivia took it to bed with her every night, hugging it as she went to sleep. It never left her bedroom. But how did it get to the landing? Olivia didn't seem surprised to see it—she dropped her mother's hand, went ahead to pick it up, and hugged it.

"Let's put it back on the bed," suggested Maria, "then it will be ready for you at sleep time."

But Olivia was still talking, "She didn't take it! She didn't take it." She allowed herself to be guided to her bedroom, the first one beyond the rear landing. There she gave the pillow a toss onto her bed.

Remembering the dinner she had been preparing, Maria picked up the child and hurried back to the kitchen. She continued, however, to think about the pillow, her daughter, and Olivia's active imagination.

At dinner that evening, Olivia was eager to tell her daddy about the girl on the stairs who was carrying her pillow. Did Daddy know the girl's name? Where did she go? Where was she now? Why did she drop the pillow? Maria caught Charles's eye and signaled him that she would explain Olivia's questions later. When she talked to Charles, Maria told him she thought their daughter had an imaginary playmate. Charles and Maria decided that Olivia had dragged the pillow from her room and then forgotten it. It wasn't a very satisfactory explanation, but what else could it be?

A few days later, Maria was busy in her bedroom—a room in front of the stair landing. Olivia was playing with two dolls, as

A child's ghost seems to have saved a life in a house that has been demolished.

she frequently did, in the wide hall at the head of the stairs. The quiet of the morning was broken by the sound of a large piece of furniture falling down the steps from the third floor, followed by a child's scream. Maria ran to the hall. Her daughter was sitting unharmed, her eyes wide.

"What happened, Mommy, who fell? Who yelled? Is it that girl again? Mommy, what fell?"

Maria picked up her daughter and held her tight. "Are you all right?" she asked over and over. She looked all round the hall, down to the landing, and even below to the first floor—but nothing was out of place. It must have been real—both of them had heard it. But Maria couldn't explain it. She took Olivia to the kitchen for a glass of juice to divert her attention.

Over the next four months, there were many times when Olivia mentioned seeing the strange girl. Once she saw her in the living room near the fireplace, another time Olivia spied the girl on the steps. When a carpool came to pick up Olivia for a trip to the nursery school, she insisted she saw the girl's face reflected in the wet glass on the front door of the house—it was a rainy morning. Then Olivia began to tell her parents about her "friend." When she looked at a picture book, she held it so her "friend" could see it too. At bedtime she wanted two glasses of water on the table—one for her "friend." Obviously Maria had no fear of the child. Charles and Maria had heard about the imaginary playmates some children acquired and decided that since Olivia was the only child in the family she created her own friend. This went on for almost a year. Then on a damp March day, Maria developed a bad headache. She dragged herself through the necessary chores and lay on the sofa in the living room so she could keep at least part of an eye on her daughter.

The television was on, playing softly to amuse Olivia who was rarely permitted to watch and was enjoying the treat. She had a few other toys there, too. Afterwards Maria couldn't recall whether or not the "friend" was there. The "friend" was never given a name (most imaginary friends are named). As soon as Charles came home, Maria asked him to take over Olivia's care— giving her dinner, a bath, and putting her to bed. Maria just wanted to go to bed herself. The aspirin she had swallowed hadn't done much good. She felt some rest might help. Maria went up to the front bedroom, put on a warm comfortable night gown, and crawled into bed in a dark, quiet room. It wasn't long before she fell asleep.

Meanwhile, Charles prepared some food for his daughter and himself. Then, following a short playtime, they retreated to the bathroom for Olivia to splash in the tub before storytime and bed. Finally Charles tucked in his daughter and her pillow, turned out the light, and moved through a short hall past the bathroom to the master bedroom. The light shining through the partially open door from the hall fell on a sleeping Maria. Charles went downstairs, gathered some study materials, and sat down on the sofa where Maria had rested earlier. The television was still playing, but it was like company.

Maria reported later that she had no idea how long she had slept or what time it was when she wakened. Charles had not come to bed. The hall light was still on, but something had wakened her. Yes, there it was again—a banging on the wall behind the head of her bed. After several raps, it came again and then again. Rousing herself more thoroughly, Maria realized the bangs must be coming from the bathroom—it was behind the wall of her room. On its other side was Olivia's room. Perhaps she was in the bathroom and needed help. Climbing out of bed, Maria went to the bathroom. The door was open, but the room was dark. Olivia could reach the light. Maria pushed the switch—no one was in there. She went on to Olivia's room. The child was sound asleep, one arm flung across her face, the other hugging the beloved pillow.

"Maybe it was pipe noise or something" Maria said to herself as she went back to bed. She barely had pulled up the covers when the banging came again, very insistently.

"Charles!" called Maria. "Are you there?"

No one answered, but the banging continued.

Again Maria slipped from the bed. Her head was better, but she still didn't feel very well. She opened the door to the hall wide and went to the head of the stairs. As she stooped to look, she could see the living room light shining into the lower hall, and she could hear the sound of the television. Charles still must be downstairs, Maria thought as she called him a couple of times. There was no answer. She began to descend the stairs. As she made the turn on the landing, an acrid smell filled her nostrils. As she continued down the stairs, leaning forward to look into the living room door to see if Charles were really there, she saw him and screamed.

Charles was sitting on the sofa with books and papers around him. While smoking a cigarette, he had fallen asleep. Some hot ashes must have dropped on the papers, smoldered, and caught fire falling onto the sofa. As Maria looked in, she saw burning sofa pieces fall onto the rug. Charles's trousers were beginning to burn, but he seemed oblivious. Maria's screams wakened him and he began to beat at the blazing seat with his hands. Tufts of the filling were falling on the rug. Maria ran in, picked up a cushion from a nearby chair, and began to beat the flames with it. As the blaze diminished, she ran to the kitchen for water to pour on everything. Within a very few minutes, the actual flames were gone, but smoke and acrid odors filled the room. Charles went to the kitchen to pour cold water over his painfully burned hands and leg.

A neighbor in the other side of the twin home heard the noise and ran to see what was wrong. As soon as the man saw Charles, he called his wife to stay with Maria while he drove Charles to a nearby emergency room for treatment. When the men returned about an hour later, Maria seemed calmed down, and she had attempted to assess the damage. Although the sofa would have to be re-covered, the marks on the rug weren't so bad.

However, Maria kept saying the same thing over and over—something about the child being real. The neighbors who came to offer sympathy assumed she was still distraught. They returned home, thinking Charles and Maria needed rest—things would be better in the morning. But Maria needed to talk to Charles.

"She wakened me! I heard her banging on the wall—listen,

she's not doing it any more! She saved your life and maybe Olivia's and mine too!"

Charles listened but wasn't sure he understood. The evening had been extremely difficult. The couple finally went to bed. After an almost sleepless night, they talked again, and they agreed that the imaginary child or someone had wakened Maria. Over the next few days, Charles and Maria asked the neighbors about former residents of the house. They learned that for approximately ten years, people moved in and out quickly, seldom staying more than a few months. But even though some people had been in the neighborhood twenty years or more, they knew virtually nothing about residents of this particular house.

About a week after the fire, Hal, an upholsterer Maria had contacted came to pick up the sofa for repair and recovering. Of course, he asked about the fire. Maria had come to expect people to look at her strangely when she explained what had happened, but this man just nodded his head as a knowing smile spread across his face.

"You've a ghost here!" he said "A real ghost, I'll bet, who likes you and wants to help you. No, that's wrong! Who has helped you."

Maria began to question Hal. He explained that he belonged to a group interested in ghosts, hauntings, and other paranormal happenings. For the next half hour, he talked with Maria, suggesting ways to discover if a child had died in the house. He felt there was a strong possibility that Olivia really did see a child and possibly that child had warned Maria of the impending danger.

Since Charles was still very much a skeptic he hired a plumber to check the bathroom and try to find the source of the banging. The search revealed nothing wrong. Charles and Maria realized that Olivia hadn't mentioned her playmate since the fateful night.

About a month after the fire, Maria answered her doorbell to find a tall man in a clerical collar standing there, hat in hand. Identifying himself as a pastor from a nearby church, he asked permission to enter. Sitting with Maria in the living room on the newly repaired sofa, he explained why he had come.

Hal, the upholstery man, had told the pastor about the fire, the apparent ghost, and the search for information about the house. The pastor explained to Maria that about ten years earlier a family of three—two parents and a daughter—rented the house. After just a few weeks, the four-year old fell against a small chest of drawers while a repairman, who had been hired to mend the chest, had gone to his truck for tools. The chest had been pulled into the small hall on the third floor where the light was better to do the repairs. As the child fell against it, the chest slid down the steps. Reaching for the chest, the child slipped and plummeted headfirst down the steps, breaking her neck. She died soon afterwards. A shaken Maria thanked the pastor for the information as she escorted him to the door.

Was this the child Olivia saw? Was it the chest she heard fall? Did the girl waken Maria? Charles, Maria, and Olivia don't have exact answers to the questions, but they never saw or heard of the child again. Although Olivia asked about the girl occasionally, she gradually seemed to forget. However, Maria and Charles have never forgotten. Whenever they look at the burn spots on the rug, they remember and give thanks to the spirit who prevented a disaster in their home.

8

City Ghosts

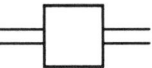

Carpenter's Hall in Philadelphia does not have a corner on ghosts in the city. Along Frankfurt Avenue there was, until recently, a home that had a monthly visitor. Until the last week of each month, it was just a normal three-bedroom row house with a small yard in the rear. But if you passed by on any of the last seven days of the month, you might see every window ablaze with light.

Mr. and Mrs. Bogar purchased the house after their last daughter was married. Mrs. Bogar wanted a small place since she used a cane when she walked, because of a back injury. It was the sixteenth of the month when the couple moved in. Within a week, they were well settled with only a few boxes left to unpack or stow and several cartons of books to be shelved. On the evening of the twenty-fourth, the Bogars started up the stairs to retire. Mrs. Bogar went first. As she reached the landing, which was only four steps from the top, she heard footsteps in the rear room at the end of the hall. Turning her head to assure herself that her husband was behind her, she said in a low voice, "Go down and call the police. Someone is in the back room." By that time Mr. Bogar heard the sounds too. Before he could retrace his steps, they both heard the door to the room open and footsteps come toward them. There was a movement of cold air as the footsteps went down the stairs past them. But no one was visible! As Mr. Bogar turned to follow the sound, he heard the steps cross the lower hall. The front door, which he had locked, opened and sounds of footsteps went outside and vanished.

By this time Mrs. Bogar was crying. "Get someone! Police or someone! Don't let him back in!" Mr. Bogar phoned the police, and a patrol car soon arrived. Two officers listened to the Bogars as they described what happened. One nodded to the other then suggested they all have some coffee or tea while the house was checked and a report was written. A short while later, promising to return the next day, the officers escorted the Bogars upstairs. As they left, they pulled the door shut and the lock slid into place.

The next afternoon the officers returned with a lady who lived nearby. The three explained to the Bogars that the visitor in their home had been heard there for years—house occupants either got used to it or moved. They were told it would occur every night for a week then stop until the next month. The only way to stop it seemed to be to leave all the lights on. Naturally the Bogars were upset to hear all this—they weren't even sure how much they believed. But they had heard the footsteps! That night, turning on every light in the house, they went to bed a little uneasily. Everything was quiet. Three or four nights later, they decided the whole thing was ridiculous, that the officers and neighbor were teasing them. So darkening the first floor, they started upstairs. It was a repetition of the first night—footsteps, movement on the steps, the open door!

The Bogars loved everything else about the house—size, location, space, so after much debate, they decided to stay. A brightly lit house was a small price. Two years later at a small party they met a lady who thought she could help them when she heard their story. The lady told the Bogars that she knew a person who contacted spirits. The medium, whose name was Janice, agreed to visit on one of the last days of the next month.

When Janice arrived at the Bogar's, she asked that the lights be dimmed. Then relaxing in an easy chair, she seemed to sleep. The footsteps started in the upstairs hall then descended the steps. As the sounds neared the door, Janice sat up and asked the person to stop and talk to her. But the steps continued, the lock and knob turned, the door opened, and whoever it was went out. The Bogars lived in the home until the row was to be demolished, but they turned on all the lights and slept with night shades the last week of the month.

In the far northeast not far from the Franklin Mills Mall is a home that was built in the 1960s. About a month after the Miles family moved in with their year-old daughter the happiness of their new home was shattered when the child became ill and died. The grief stricken parents considered moving, but they felt tied to the place. They kept the door to their daughter's room closed and everything inside the same as it was when they lovingly arranged it for her.

About three years later, a son, Alvin, was welcomed by the Miles. They completely refurnished their daughter's room for the new arrival, but they left the books the little girl had been given. Until the baby was about two, everything was normal. One day the little boy was in his room playing with some toys on the floor. Very quietly a book a board picture book of children moved from the bookcase to a place on the floor beside the youngster. He watched as the pages turned. His mother, who had been folding clean clothes, was dumbstruck. She grabbed the child and raced from the room, slamming the door behind them.

When her husband returned, she told him what had happened, trying unsuccessfully not to panic. He slowly opened the door. The book was still on the floor. John tried to reassure his wife. Slowly she regained her composure. Maybe Alvin had pulled down the book when she wasn't looking. Days later, Alvin was playing with a truck when he pulled it close to his chest and began slapping at an invisible something and shouting, "No! No!"

During the next few years, Alvin developed an imaginary playmate. He talked to her, argued with her, wanted a place at the table for her, and carried out all the activities that children with imaginary friends do. As it neared time for Alvin to attend kindergarten, the invisible friend appeared less and less.

On a visit to his grandparents, Alvin saw a picture of his sister. Picking it up, he kissed it and said she wasn't coming any more. You can imagine his parents shocked reaction.

In the 1970s the family was transferred to Cleveland. One day they received a letter from the new owner of the home asking if a child had died in the middle room. Their four- year-old twin girls, who now used the room, insisted a small girl toddled around and wanted to play with them.

A third family who lives there now has experienced similar activity. Apparently the Miles' daughter is still there.

In Chestnut Hill, Baleroy, the home of George Gordon Meade Easby, is reported to be haunted. Many guests have listened to his report of ghosts and seen photographs of rooms containing not only rare and beautiful antiques but also ectoplasm—that's defined as "an emanation from a spiritualist medium that is believed to effect telekinesis and similar phenomena." Ectoplasm is said to exist only when a ghost or spirit is present. Easby assured his guests, at a party in 1984 that he and one of his household employees had seen a ghost or two before the guests arrived.

According to Meade Easby, it can be a truly fatal mistake to sit in a certain blue chair. To some it has meant unexpected, imminent death. According to Mr. Easby that was the fate of a housekeeper, a cousin, and two friends of his. And there's a story of a tape recorder being thrown across a bedroom when a reporter attempted to use it.

Baleroy, its antiques, ghosts, and host add color to Chestnut Hill.

On the southern part of the city, where Philadelphia and Darby meet, there is a charming old stone building called the Blue Bell Inn. It was here that Washington was first welcomed to

Philadelphia and also where he gave his last farewell. Mary Beth Lauer, a newspaper reporter in Delaware County, talked with June Sams who now lives in the Inn built in 1766 and has reported some of the inn's history.

Blue Bell Tavern, scene of a small battle, used to be on the very edge of Philadelphia. Washington passed by here.

In November, 1777 a battle between the British and the American patriots took place in front of the Inn. Only one British soldier was slain there (although five patriots met the same fate), and as he died, he lamented "Now I will never leave this accursed land!"

According to Sams, the soldier is still there. Apparently his ghost is trying to figure out what her answering machine does because he seems to play with it, and although he likes to take things, he eventually puts them back. Sams has seen his britches and boots; the rest of the figure is obscured in a white mist.

There's a cat ghost in center city. Her name, Ebony, was given to her because she was a handsome glossy black. She was never permitted outside, living with her owners Paul and Vi in a Seventeenth Street third-floor apartment. Through her life, the only time Ebony left home was for periodic checks at the veterinarian. She also stayed at his office for two weeks every summer when her owners went on vacation. At the age of fourteen, she caught cold, became very ill, and died within a few days. The vet disposed of her body for the grieving owners.

Paul and Vi left in June, three months later, for their vacation. On their return, the resident of the first floor apartment spoke to them as they entered the hall to go up stairs.

"Your cat is in here," he said. "She was crying outside this morning. I was worried she'd be stolen, or hurt, or something, so I brought her in. I'll get her."

Paul and Vi stared at each other. What was he talking about? It certainly wasn't their cat! The man returned saying he couldn't find her but would bring her up when he did. To add further to the mystery, when they entered the apartment, Ebony's favorite pillow had been dragged to the corner where she'd liked it. Their bed had a small hollow near the foot, just where the cat always had made one.

Later in the evening, the first floor tenant phoned to report he hadn't found the cat—she must have slipped out. Thanking him profusely, they assured him she was fine.

Ever since, they find evidence that Ebony is still around. Even when they put her pillow in a drawer somehow it finds its way to the corner—now they just leave it there.

9

Mainline Hauntings

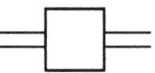

pparitions of all kinds have been attributed to the Main Line area and its neighbors. The General Wayne Inn, undoubtedly the most famous, is not the only place with a haunting. In Rosemont, there's a house with a ghost horse as well as its rider nearby. The house is located on what is now a small lot, although when it was new, there was much ground around it. Once in a while, there seems to be the sound of a horse galloping toward the house. Hundreds of automobiles pass the place every day but not horses. The hoofbeats pound up the driveway then stop suddenly. Within moments, the residents hear a banging on the front door. When the door is opened no one is there. This occurred frequently in the past, but recently it inexplicably has diminished.

One research group brought a psychic named Edward to the home, by invitation of course. He wasn't told what had happened—just that there seemed to be a problem. After strolling around the walk, the driveway, and the first floor rooms, Edward sat down on a low stool near the entrance. He was quiet for about fifteen minutes. Those present were quiet, also, waiting to see what would happen. Finally Edward began to speak. He said he was seeing a horse and rider coming through a wooded area in a bad storm. "No," he corrected himself, "there are two horses and riders." In his mind's eye, he reported, he saw one rider fall from a rearing, terrified horse, frightened by the thunder and lightning. The other man rode on to this house, the nearest place seeking help. When no one responded to his banging on the door, he returned to the injured man, dragged him to the house, pushed open the door, and pulled the now unconscious companion inside out of the weather. But the man died almost immediately. The rider then told Edward the date when it happened. Later when records were searched, they indicated that the house was unoccupied at that time.

A well known writer who lived in the house as a preteenager remembers hearing the horse, particularly on some stormy nights. His mother told him it was like the highwayman that Robert Louis Stevenson wrote about, but he knew he heard a horse. No one has reported hearing the horse for about five years.

Bob Goshorn has described some other Main Line ghosts in an article entitled "Five Tales for All Hallow's Even." Included among the specters is that of Priscilla Moore Robinson, known as Prissy, one of the most famous ghosts of the area. She lived a hundred years (1777 to 1877) and for much of that time she ran (with a rough hand) the Blue Bell Tavern, now a private home not far from the Daylesford Station. According to Goshorn, well-known residents of the former Inn, including Mary Croasdale, the director of the County Department of Public Assistance and the first Republican committee woman in Tredyffrin Township, has reported hearing knockings on door and windows. Bureau drawers have opened with no apparent cause. Curtains have rustled when there was no breeze. Mrs. Croasdale has felt the touch of a hand on her arm or shoulder.

Prissy's Home on the Main Line is now a private dwelling.

Mary Croasdale lived at the inn for nearly 58 years and referred to it as having a "reputation for being haunted" in a history she wrote. Other people who have lived there, including Dick

Ferguson, a fine arts dealer and Paul M. Warner, editorial page director of the Philadelphia Inquirer. All have related their experiences with Prissy.

Evidence of the violence that took place in the tavern was uncovered when six skeletons were found on the premises in the garden that was being installed in the rear of the house. Were they visitors or workers? It is suspected that they were peddlers, drovers, or traders who either flashed too much money or were on the losing end of a brawl. Prissy must have known about their demise. She may even have had a hand in the deaths. Prissy married three times and was a hard-headed lady. She had to be to manage the noisy, quarreling crew who traveled the road from Lancaster to Philadelphia. According to the tales about her, she even threatened the crews of the trains passing by. When a train killed one of her calves and she demanded payment, the railroad refused. She then greased the rails with animal fat and soon afterwards was recompensed for her loss.

As Prissy aged, she sprouted white whiskers which made her appear fearsome, especially to children. This only added to the stories of her meanness. When she died she was a difficult, cantankerous old lady. Her rest has not been peaceful.

Jeffries, in her book on ghosts, reports that a photograph was taken when a house near the old Inn (which originally was part of the property) burned. The picture was intended to show a wall bearing the outline of stair treads. However, when it was developed, the photograph included an old woman in a big bonnet. No trick of light to create such an illusion could be found. Some people believed it was Prissy.

Although she is the most disagreeable, Prissy is not the only Main Line ghost. Several times, Dr. Anthony Wayne Baugh, surgeon for the Pennsylvania Railroad and a school director for Tredyffrin School District, has reported seeing the ghost of a colonial soldier riding a horse. Of course, others have seen him too, but Dr. Baugh had a reputation for scoffing at the occult.

The soldier was part of a detachment encamped near Paoli in September, 1777 to watch the British army and to report to General Wayne, their commander, signs that the British were preparing to cross the Schuylkill River and move on Philadelphia. Since he lived nearby, this soldier returned home nightly so the army didn't have to feed him. One night he had a dream that his fellow soldiers were being slaughtered. It was so real it awakened him. Returning to sleep, he continued his dream. He awoke again, but this time he hastened to join his company. On arriving at the camp, he found many of his comrades dead, but before he could flee, he was beheaded. On the anniversary of the massacre he rides through Paoli. Those who've seen him vow the horses hooves are silent. They also suggest that if you see him, you should look away quickly. For if he notices your stares, he will remove his head and give it to you (a sure sign you will join him before a year passes).

The soldier's commander, General Wayne, is reported to be seen riding his great horse, Nab, near the Brandywine Battle field, at the site of the massacre, and near Fort Ticonderoga in the Hudson River Valley. The general and his ghost horse do seem to move around!

Goshorn and others have reported the story of Hannah Wayne who accidentally burned to death. The lady lived in Waynesborough in the Civil War era. One day, she climbed through a small trap door leading to the attic of her home. The candle she was carrying set fire to her clothing. As she tried to beat out the flames and cry for help, she broke the nearby windows with her feet. The men of the house were too far away in the fields to hear her; and although the women in the nearby garden heard her pleas, they were unable to reach her in time and she died.

Since then women, never men, have heard glass breaking. At a dinner party the ladies may hear a shattering sound, but no broken glass is ever found. The householders believe it is Hannah Wayne.

A famous old mansion, used to stand seventeen miles west of Philadelphia. That's not really the Main Line, but near enough to be noted here. Its history is recorded in a book, *Night Stalks the Mansion* by Harold Cameron and Constance Westbie. Cameron's unsuspecting family of seven moved into the mansion only to learn through sad experience that it was haunted by the ghost of a rapist/murderer and the mother of his victim. The place was destroyed by fire but lives on in this very popular nonfiction report of one family's unsettling experiences as they tried to discover who inhabited the house with them.

Other areas of Delaware County have their share of haunted places, from a house on Valleybrook Road in Glen Mills (where nothing has been seen, but voices and footsteps have been heard for years) to a tavern in Newtown Square (which was the site of the final robbery committed by a highwayman known as Sandy Flash). He was hanged in Chester for this and other crimes.

Jane Wagner of Havertown tells how the entity in her home, a renovated carriage house originally built in 1730, locked her out three times the first week she lived there. Her husband, Graham, had to return from his office on each occasion to let her in. The screen door locked with a plunger that had to be pushed into place; it just didn't fall. The Wagners had no children at that time so that explanation was eliminated. Jane hasn't been locked out since that first week, although there is other evidence of an unseen visitor.

One of the most unique events occurred when Jane was pregnant with her third child. It was customary for each family member to prepare his or her own breakfast. Cereals were stored in a specific drawer, fruit, juice, and milk in the refrigerator. Other items were nearby. About 5:30 in the morning, Jane would be wakened by the sound of breakfast preparations—dishes being pulled from the cupboards and placed on the table, the clatter of silver, cereal boxes ripping open, and other suitable sounds. When she entered the kitchen, no one was there, everything was in its proper storage place, nothing was disturbed. No explanation has been found.

The Wagners have experienced a phenomenon that owners of cats and haunted houses often have to deal with. Because of the unusual floor plan of the house, the cat's litter box is kept in the attic at the top of a small staircase. On most days of the month, the cat trots up the steps, uses the box, and quietly returns downstairs. However, on the night of the full moon, even if its cloudy or storming, after the cat uses the box during the night, she clears the steps with one leap, races into the master bedroom, and, with her fur on end, emits an unearthly howl. If the Wagners are asleep when this begins, they leap from their bed.

A family in Valley Forge also has a problem with their cat when the moon is full. The animal leaps and howls as though something or someone is chasing her. After an hour, she stops and settles down for another month. One month her gyrations broke an antique clock. (That didn't please her owners.)

The experience of cats misbehaving in haunted places is a familiar one. Similar activity is reported all over the world. Dogs generally show fear and cringe when an entity seems to be present. One dog even killed himself when he saw a ghost.

A home in Wayne is reputed to be haunted by an elderly lady. As far as the owners of the carriage house can tell, she only rearranges the dishes and table linen and scatters them about the house. When that occurs, the family just gathers and returns them to the proper places.

10

Bucks County Entities

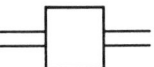

The upper part of the Delaware Valley has many ghosts. One resident has remarked that at homes and inns all along the old Delaware Canal you'll find ghosts of every era from Revolutionary days to modern times. Walking tours in the New Hope community have featured haunted places and, hopefully, specters.

The ghosts of Logan Inn in New Hope, on the corner of Main and Ferry Streets have been described in several books. The authors report the details of a portrait which was moved from the beautiful dining room to a stairway because the scent of lavender that comes from the portrait used to bother diners.

Locked doors are opened, a mirror is covered with soap like spatters, a witch's ball has mysteriously appeared and just as mysteriously left. People who lived in the area in the 40s relate a tale that concerns the parking lot of the Inn. In July 1946, the annual street fair was held on the parking lot and the tow path adjoining it. Parker Dehn, the husband of Henrietta Cunningham who owned the nearby Tow Path House, was acting as a Swami Rajah and reading palms in a tent pitched on the Tow Path. Other townspeople were contributing to the fun by displaying acts of skill, crafts, or amusements.

On Thursday, the first evening, Parker had read the fortunes of several patrons when the hysterical crying of a child filled his tent. It was so loud and distracting that Parker went outside to request that the child be removed from the area. But no crying youngster of any size could be found, and the sound had ceased. As soon as Parker reentered the tent, it began again. And again Dehn looked for the child fruitlessly. Even customers waiting their turns for a fortune heard the sobbing but couldn't locate it. After Parker unsuccessfully tried a third time to read one young lady's palm, he stormed out of the tent, told those waiting to go away, and headed for the hotel bar.

Friday night the same thing occurred. The sobbing and screaming started during the third reading and continued until Parker again retreated to the bar for a calming drink. However, this time several artists working nearby sketching portraits of fair goers heard the noise. The local police officer and constable were called, but they could not find the source of the annoyance, so the artists packed their materials and joined Parker. Saturday night was a repetition. After an hour or so, as the fair area darkened, there was no palm reader. The astrologer moved to the bar, as did several artists and food vendors. The bar was doing a good business. After the fair closed, no one heard the weeping and screaming until the next year, 1947.

That year was a repetition of the previous July. By Saturday night, curiosity seekers came to hear the noise and try to locate its source but without luck. So in 1948, there was no fair. Instead, an auction was held in the Canal by the Tow Path House (There was no water then in that part of the Canal.) St. John Terrell, later of Lambertville Music Circus fame, served as auctioneer. There was no crying, screaming or sobbing. What was the crying that was so disturbing it ended an annual event? Some people claim it was caused by a child who fell and drowned. Others think it came from a ghost child who saw a parent fall from a boat in the water. To date, no one really knows what happened, but some folks insist they still hear the crying.

Not far from New Hope some people have reported seeing the ghost known as Midnight Mary from Bristol. Mary had attended her school prom on a lovely late spring night. Wearing a soft pink dress, she danced and had a splendid time. On the way home the young driver who escorted her lost control of the car; it fell into Tullytown Lake. Mary's body was never recovered. People in the area—a mother wheeling a carriage, strollers along the shore—see her dance on the water, then disappear.

Lucy, another teenager ghost, was the result of an accident on Route 202 not far from Norristown. She had been hitchhiking when a driver picked her up. A short time later, the car was hit head on and Lucy was killed instantly. Since then, many drivers on that stretch of road see a young girl thumbing a ride. When someone picks her up, she sits quietly on the front seat for several miles. When the driver asks her a question, or glances her way, the passenger seat is empty. Hitchhiking ghosts have been seen in many communities.

An old home nearby has a music loving ghost—she is the ghost of a young woman who was studying to be a concert pianist when she died of tuberculosis. Years later, Alan, a student musician visited the house. As he arrived, accompanying a friend stopping there on business, he announced that he had been told the house was haunted, but he didn't believe in ghosts. His friend and their hostess offered to show the young man some interesting features of the house. They came to a room containing two pianos. The student asked permission to play for the young woman sitting in an easy chair. The hostess and the friend, looking toward the chair, saw no one. But Alan insisted, and began to play a Chopin prelude. Several times he smiled toward the chair as he played. When he finished, he turned to the chair, thanked whoever he saw sitting there, then rejoined the pair waiting in the next room. They didn't tell him the young lady had died years before, and Chopin had been her favorite composer. It's easy to imagine their surprise when he remarked, as he entered the car, "Tell Charlene I'll be back and will play for her again."

The lady's name had been Charlene.

Just to the north of Willow Grove is a small park and historical house known as Graeme Park. The beautiful old home has been a residence for many and is in good condition. A visitor may be told that several nights a year a young woman may be seen moving slowly across the lawn from the house toward a pond. In colonial days, the young daughter of the house fell in love with the son of Benjamin Franklin, but was rejected by him.

Tucked along the highways and byways of the Delaware Valley

are the scenes of many more tales of spirits and hauntings. Perhaps you pass by such a place every day. Who knows who among us will be next to join the hauntings?

New Hope's Logan Inn. A famous ghostly occurrence includes the scent of lavender emanating from a picture.

Bibliography

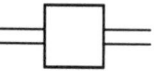

Jeffrey, Adi-Kent Thomas. *Ghosts in the Valley.* New Hope Art Shop, 1971.

Rausher, William. *The Spiritual Frontier.* Doubleday, 1975.

Roberts, Bruce and Mancy. *America's Most Haunted Places.* Doubleday, 1976.

Westbie, Constable and Harold, Cameron. *Night Stalks the Mansion.* Stackpole, 1978.

In Search of Ghosts
Haunted Places in the
Delaware Valley

Elizabeth P. Hoffman

If you cannot find this book at your local bookstore, it can be ordered directly from the publisher at:

CAMINO BOOKS, INC.
P.O. Box 59026
Philadelphia, PA 19102

Please send me:

____copy(ies) of *In Search of Ghosts* ($7.95)
(please add $2.00 for postage & handling)

Name _____

Address _____

City/State/Zip _____

All orders must be prepaid. Your satisfaction is guaranteed. You can return the book for a full refund.

14-7